# Accounts Preparation Wise Guide

## AAT Level 3 Diploma in Accounting



Published by Osborne Books Limited, Unit 1B Everoak Estate, Bromyard Road, Worcester WR2 5HP
Tel 01905 748071, Email books@osbornebooks.co.uk, Website www.osbornebooks.co.uk

Printed and bound by Mimeo, UK.

ISBN 978 1909173 446

# how to use this Wise Guide

This Wise Guide has been designed to supplement your Tutorial and Workbook. It has two main aims:

- to reinforce your learning as you study your course
- to help you prepare for your online assessment

This Wise Guide is organised in the specific topic areas listed on pages 4 and 5. These individual topic areas have been designed to cover the main areas of study, concentrating on specific areas of difficulty. There is also an index at the back to help you find the areas you are studying or revising.

The Owl symbolises wisdom, and acts as your tutor, introducing and explaining topics. Please let us know if he is doing his job properly. If you have feedback on this material please email books@osbornebooks.co.uk

Thank you and good luck with your study and revision.

Osborne Books

## REVISION TIPS

*'**OWL**' stands for:* ***O****bserve* ***W****rite* ***L****earn*

*There are a number of well-known ways in which you can remember information:*

- *You can remember what it looks like on the page. Diagrams, lists, mind-maps, colour coding for different types of information, all help you **observe** and remember.*
- *You can remember what you **write** down. Flash cards, post-it notes around the bathroom mirror, notes on a mobile phone all help. It is the process of writing which fixes the information in the brain.*
- *You can **learn** by using this Wise Guide. Read through each topic carefully and then prepare your own written version on flash cards, post-it notes, wall charts – anything that you can see regularly.*
- *Lastly, give yourself **chill out** time, your brain a chance to recover and the information time to sink in. Promise yourself treats when you have finished studying – a drink, chocolate, a work out. Relax! And pass.*

# list of contents

# 1 Accounting records

***INTRODUCTION***

*You know from your studies that accounting is all about recording financial information and looking after it. You need to be able to understand – and be able to explain – why accounting requires such precision and rigorous attention to detail.*

## accounting records should be:

- **accurate** – entered correctly and regularly checked using reconciliation and checking techniques, eg bank reconciliation, subsidiary ledger reconciliation, production of trial balance
- **up-to-date** – updated daily from available sources of information
- **secure** – kept safely and stored for the requisite period of time (6 years from the end of the current financial year)
- **confidential** – only available to authorised individuals

## the accounting system flow

| | |
|---|---|
| **source documents** | invoices, bank statements |
| ↓ **books of prime entry** | day books, cash book, journal |
| ↓ **double-entry accounts** | general ledger, cash book, sales and purchases ledgers |
| ↓ **trial balance** | list of general ledger account balances |
| ↓ **financial statements** | statement of profit or loss, statement of financial position |

## books of prime entry

These feature in the accounting flow and list details from source documents as follows:

- **sales day book** — sales invoices issued to credit customers
- **sales returns day book** — sales credit notes issued to credit customers
- **purchases day book** — purchase invoices received from credit suppliers
- **purchases returns day book** — purchase credit notes received from credit suppliers
- **cash book** — details of cash and bank receipts and payments
- **journal** — details of non-regular transactions

## double-entry: division of the ledger

| ledger | accounts |
|---|---|
| general ledger | assets, expenses, sales, purchases |
| cash book* | cash and bank |
| sales ledger (usually subsidiary**) | individual customer accounts |
| purchases ledger (usually subsidiary**) | individual supplier accounts |

**Notes**

* The **cash book** can be both a book of prime entry and part of double-entry, or it can be just a book of prime entry represented in the general ledger by cash and bank control accounts.

** **'Subsidiary'** means 'not part of the general ledger'. The sales and purchases ledger are represented in the general ledger by control accounts.

## other accounting records

- **inventory records**: to monitor and control movement of inventory in and out of the business
- **asset register**: to record and monitor acquisition, depreciation and disposal of non-current assets

## why keep accounts?

- **for internal control**
  - – to monitor cash flow - how much is owed to and by the business at any time
  - – to assist management in decision-making, eg investments, staffing, cut-backs
  - – to prevent the possibility of fraud, eg theft of money or goods from the business
- **to measure business performance**
  - – to find out whether the business is profitable by regular reporting, eg periodic and year-end financial statements
  - – to compare one period's results with another or with another organisation
- **to obtain credit or finance - loans and credit accounts**
  - – to provide evidence to banks, other lenders and suppliers that the business is sound and can repay the borrowing
- **to comply with legal (statutory) requirements, eg**
  - – submission of VAT returns
  - – submission of income tax returns

# 2 Accounting equation and double-entry

***KEEPING BALANCE***

*The accounting equation is central to the way we keep accounting records and produce financial statements. It is always central to ensuring the accuracy of the statement of financial position which contains the various elements of the accounting equation.*

## the accounting equation

**assets**

*the value of . . .*
non-current assets
+
current assets

*minus*

**liabilities**

*the value of . . .*
non-current liabilities
+
current liabilities

*equals*

**capital**

*the value of . . .*
opening capital
+ capital introduced
+ profit
– drawings

# accounting equation – some definitions

## ASSETS

**non-current assets:**
Items bought for use within the business which have a useful life of more than a year, eg machinery, vehicles, furniture, equipment. These are classified as **tangible** (having material substance, touchable) or **intangible** (not touchable), eg goodwill, trademarks.

**current assets:**
Items needed for everyday use within the business that will be used or will change within a year, eg inventory, trade receivables, money. Also includes the value of prepaid expenses and accrued income.

## LIABILITIES

**non-current liabilities:**
Long-term debts repayable beyond one year, eg bank loans, mortgages.

**current liabilities:**
Short-term debt repayable within a year, eg trade payables, bank overdraft, VAT and payroll taxes due to HMRC. Also includes prepaid income and accrued expenses.

## CAPITAL

Money invested by the owner(s) *plus* profits (or *minus* losses) to date, *minus* any money withdrawn (drawings).

## how the accounting equation works

A change in values in any part of the accounting equation may alter the totals, but the equation should always balance, as seen below:

**Example**: a business purchases shop fittings on credit; they cost for £5,000 plus VAT. The accounting equation will change as follows:

| **Assets** | *minus* | **Liabilities** | *equals* | **Capital** |
|---|---|---|---|---|
| £ | | £ | | £ |
| 80,000 | – | 60,000 | = | 20,000 |
| + £5,000 | | + £6,000 (payables) | | |
| | | – 1,000 (VAT) | | |
| 85,000 | – | 65,000 | = | 20,000 |

Also, the elements of the accounting equation can be moved around so that any element can be calculated if the other two are known, for example (using the above figures):

| **example:** | **capital** | *plus* | **liabilities** | *equals* | **assets** |
|---|---|---|---|---|---|
| | £20,000 | + | £60,000 | = | £80,000 |

| **example:** | **assets** | *minus* | **capital** | *equals* | **liabilities** |
|---|---|---|---|---|---|
| | £80,000 | – | £20,000 | = | £60,000 |

**owner capital 'mini' equation**

As illustrated on pages 10 and 11, the Capital section in a sole trader statement of financial position contains a mini-equation which summarises movement in owner capital during the period. The elements (with sample figures) are:

**Opening capital** £80,000 + **Capital introduced** £20,000 + **Profit for the period** £100,000 *minus* **Drawings** £30,000 *equals* **Closing capital** £170,000.

Where any one figure is missing it can be calculated using simple maths:

**Example 1: the Capital introduced figure is missing:**

| Opening capital | + | Capital introduced | + | Profit for the period | – | Drawings | = | Closing capital |
|---|---|---|---|---|---|---|---|---|
| £80,000 | + | **£????** | + | £100,000 | – | £30,000 | = | £170,000 |

**Workings**: £170,000 + £30,000 – £100,000 – £80,000 = Capital introduced is £20,000

**Example 2: the Drawings figure is missing:**

| Opening capital | + | Capital introduced | + | Profit for the period | – | Drawings | = | Closing capital |
|---|---|---|---|---|---|---|---|---|
| £80,000 | + | £20,000 | + | £100,000 | – | **£????** | = | £170,000 |

**Workings**: £80,000 + £20,000 + £100,000 – £170,000 = Drawings are £30,000

## double-entry principles – a reminder

The accounting equation depends on correct double-entry of accounting transactions. Here is a quick reminder of double-entry rules:

For every transaction there are two entries in the accounts for the same amount:

- **one is on the debit (left) side of an account**
- **the other is on the credit (right) side**

### debit or credit?

Sometimes it is difficult to remember which items are debits and which are credits. The decision on which entry goes on which side is based on the following principles:

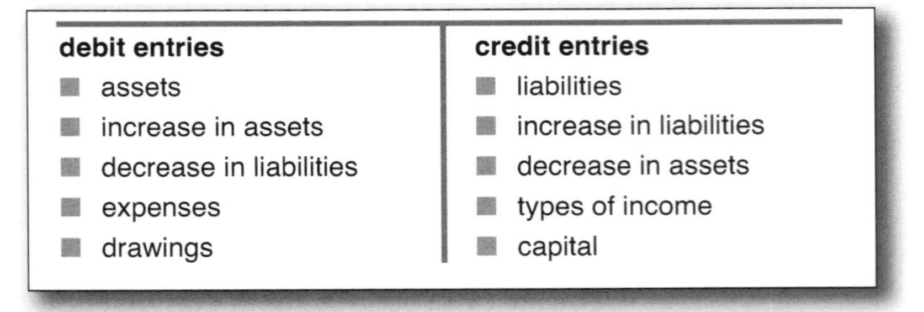

| debit entries | credit entries |
|---|---|
| assets | liabilities |
| increase in assets | increase in liabilities |
| decrease in liabilities | decrease in assets |
| expenses | types of income |
| drawings | capital |

## financial statements – an introduction

The next chapter explains how to allocate the balances of the double-entry accounts from the trial balance to the financial statements. So that you can appreciate fully what is going on in this process you will need to be aware of the information the financial statements provide for the business owner. There are two financial statements involved:

- **statement of profit or loss**

  This calculates the revenue (income) and expenses of the business over a set period of time (usually the financial year) and the profit (or loss) for that period.

- **statement of financial position**

  This sets out the figures you will be familiar with from the accounting equation (see pages 10-12). It shows the owner what the business is worth at any one time.

**assets**
non-current assets + current assets (what the business owns)

*minus*

**liabilities**
non-current liabilities + current liabilities (what the business owes)

*equals*

**capital**
investment of the owner (what the business is worth)

# 3 The extended trial balance

## *TRIAL BALANCES – THE DIFFERENT TYPES*

*Extracting a trial balance from the general ledger provides a check on whether the double entry is accurate. In the preparation of financial statements – the statement of profit or loss (SPL) and the statement of financial position (SFP) – the initial trial balance (ITB) is used as a starting point for the extended trial balance (ETB).*

## some definitions

**initial trial balance (ITB)**
A list of the balances of every account in the general ledger, including the cash book, on the last day of a financial period. It lists debit balances and credit balances in separate columns and shows a total for each column. The two totals should be the same value.

**extended trial balance (ETB)**
A method of assigning balances from the initial trial balance to their respective financial statements:

- the statement of profit or loss, or
- the statement of financial position

Period end adjustments can be included.

## Extended Trial Balance (ETB) format

| *General ledger account* | *Initial trial balance - general ledger account balances* | | *Adjustments ** | | *Statement of Profit or Loss* | | *Statement of Financial Position* | |
|---|---|---|---|---|---|---|---|---|
| | Dr | Cr | Dr | Cr | Dr | Cr | Dr | Cr |
| A row for each account name | Value £ | Value £ | Value £ | Value £ | Value £ | Value £ | Value £ | Value £ |
| | | | | | | | | |
| Totals | A | = A | B | = B | C | = C | D | = D |

**Enter period-end adjustments:**

- accruals
- prepayments
- closing inventory
- depreciation
- irrecoverable debts
- allowance for doubtful debts

**Checking the bottom row totals:**

If the correct double-entry has been carried out, the totals of every pair of columns will balance,

so . . .

A = A, B = B, C = C, D = D

## how does the ETB work?

Combined values from the initial trial balance and the adjustments columns are extended to the appropriate financial statement columns. You should start working from the left and move towards the right, as shown below.

### EXAMPLE – ETB extract

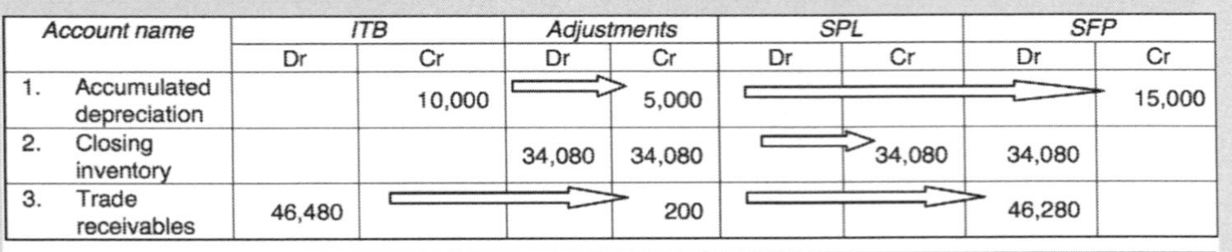

| Account name | ITB | | Adjustments | | SPL | | SFP | |
|---|---|---|---|---|---|---|---|---|
| | Dr | Cr | Dr | Cr | Dr | Cr | Dr | Cr |
| 1. Accumulated depreciation | | 10,000 | | 5,000 | | | | 15,000 |
| 2. Closing inventory | | | 34,080 | 34,080 | | 34,080 | 34,080 | |
| 3. Trade receivables | 46,480 | | | 200 | | | 46,280 | |

1. Accumulated depreciation (credit) of £10,000 from the ITB is adjusted upwards by £5,000 (credit) for the current year, and the combined total £15,000 (credit) extended to the SFP.

2. Closing inventory of £34,080 is entered in the period-end adjustments column as both a debit and a credit. These are then extended to the SPL (credit) and the SFP (debit).

3. Trade receivables (debit) of £46,480 from the ITB is adjusted downwards by £200 (credit) for the current year and the combined total £46,280 (debit) is extended to the SFP.

## EXAMPLE – fully displayed ETB

| *Account name* | *ITB* | | *Adjustments ** | | *SPL* | | *SFP* | |
|---|---|---|---|---|---|---|---|---|
| | Dr | Cr | Dr | Cr | Dr | Cr | Dr | Cr |
| Sales | | 243,820 | | | | 243,820 | | |
| Opening inventory | 30,030 | | | | 30,030 | | | |
| Purchases | 140,950 | | | | 140,950 | | | |
| Cls inventory SPL | | | | 34,080 | | 34,080 | | |
| General expenses | 55,065 | | 940 | 220 | 55,785 | | | |
| Depreciation | | | 5,000 | | 5,000 | | | |
| Loss on disposal | 850 | | | | 850 | | | |
| Irrecoverable debt | | | 200 | | 200 | | | |
| Fittings | 30,000 | | | | | | 30,000 | |
| Accum dep'n | | 10,000 | | 5,000 | | | | 15,000 |
| Cls inventory SFP | | | 34,080 | | | | 34,080 | |
| Trade receivables | 46,480 | | | 200 | | | 46,280 | |
| Prepayment (exp) | | | 220 | | | | 220 | |
| Cash and bank | 10,180 | | | | | | 10,180 | |
| Trade payables | | 24,930 | | | | | | 24,930 |
| VAT | | 3,860 | | | | | | 3,860 |
| Accrual (expense) | | | | 940 | | | | 940 |
| Capital | | 62,000 | | | | | | 62,000 |
| Drawings | 31,055 | | | | | | 31,055 | |
| Profit or loss | | | | | * 45,085 | | | * 45,085 |
| **Totals** | **344,610** | **344,610** | **40,440** | **40,440** | **277,900** | **277,900** | **151,815** | **151,815** |

* The entry of £45,085 forces the SPL columns to balance. It is then entered as a credit in the SFP.

## calculation of profit or loss using the ETB

This page shows the entries in the ETB columns for the statement of profit or loss (SPL) and the statement of financial position (SFP) and their treatment in the accounts.

| *Other columns of ETB* | *Statement of profit or loss* | | *Statement of financial position* | |
|---|---|---|---|---|
| | Dr | Cr | Dr | Cr |
| ⇨ | Value £ | Value £ | Value £ | Value £ |
| | **Y** | **Z** | **Z** | **Y** |
| | Total | Total | Total | Total |

**step 1**

After the values are listed in the ETB, enter a new figure here to make the Dr and Cr columns in the SPL balance.

- *a debit entry represents a profit (**Y**)*
- *a credit entry represents a loss (**Z**)*

The SPL is a 'T' account and therefore part of double-entry. **Y** and **Z** are carried down balances.

**step 2**

The brought down balance from the SPL is shown in the SFP, so is re-written here in the ETB.

- *a credit balance represents a profit (**Y**)*
- *a debit balance represents a loss (**Z**)*

The SFP is a snapshot of the accounting equation on the last day of the period. **Y** and **Z** are increases or decreases in owner capital.

## important points to remember when using the ETB

- The order of account names in the ETB will not follow any particular pattern. It could be alphabetical, roughly grouped by account type or, most likely, completely random.
- Cost of sales may be given as a net figure in the trial balance (ITB). In that case, there will be no entry for opening inventory, purchases or closing inventory in the SPL (statement of profit or loss). There will still be a debit entry for closing inventory which belongs in the SFP (statement of financial position).
- Discount allowed (an expense and so a debit) and Discount received (a type of income and so a credit) belong in the SPL.
- Profit (gain) or loss on the sale of non-current assets belongs in the SPL.
- Drawings account is extended to the SFP. It is a reduction in owner capital, not an expense of the business.
- A VAT account balance belongs in the SFP and will normally be a credit – a liability.
- Cash kept within the business extends to the SFP and can only be a debit (an asset).
- A bank overdraft is a credit in the SFP – a liability to pay back short-term borrowing from the bank.

## which account balances and adjustments are extended to the SPL?

- **income accounts**:
  Sales revenue, Interest received, Discount received, Profit on disposal of non-current assets
- **cost of sales:**
  opening inventory + purchases – closing inventory = Cost of sales
- **day-to-day expenses:**
  everyday running costs of the business, eg administration expenses, advertising and promotion, electricity, rent and rates, interest paid, discount allowed
- **periodic charges or expenses:**
  depreciation charge, loss on disposal of non-current assets; irrecoverable debts, allowance for doubtful debts adjustment
- **calculation of net profit (or loss):**
  the carried down balance of the SPL columns seen as a 'T' account

**Note:** all 'T' accounts associated with the SPL return to a zero balance for the start of the new period because all balances will have been moved to the statement of profit or loss (except those with accruals or prepayments carried down).

## Which account balances and adjustments are extended to the SFP?

- **assets:**

  *Non-current assets:* carrying amount (or net book value), ie original cost less accumulated depreciation

  *Current assets:* closing inventory, trade receivables (Sales ledger control account) less allowance for doubtful debts, insurance claim, prepayment of expenses, accrual of income, bank and cash

- **liabilities:**

  *Current liabilities:* trade payables (Purchases ledger control account), VAT and other taxes, accrual of expenses, prepayment of income

  *Non-current liabilities:* loans or amounts due for repayment in more than a year

- **capital:**
  Opening capital *plus* capital introduced during the period *plus* profit generated during the period (or *minus* the loss incurred during the period) *minus* Drawings = Closing capital

**Note:** all 'T' accounts associated with the SFP are ongoing, ie they continue into the next period. The statement of financial position can be said to show **"what the business owns and what the business owes at any one point in time."**

# 4 Accruals and prepayments

## *UNDERSTANDING THE ACCRUALS CONCEPT*

*The end-of-period adjustments can be some of the trickiest areas of accounts preparation.*

*They are made necessary because of the* ***accruals concept*** *in accounting.*

### the accruals concept

The accruals concept is all to do with timing:

- **Income** for accounting purposes is recognised at the point of time when it is **earned** rather than when the money is received
- **Expenses** for accounting purposes are recognised at the point of time when they are **incurred** rather than when the money is paid

# accruals and prepayments – some definitions

### types of accrual

- **Accrued expense** is an expense which has been incurred in an accounting period but has not yet been paid at the end of it, eg a power bill for gas used.
- **Accrued income** is income which has been earned in an accounting period but has not yet been received at the end of it, eg commission due on sales.

### types of prepayment

- **Prepaid expense** is an expense which has been paid for in an accounting period but relates to a later accounting period, eg office rent paid quarterly in advance.
- **Prepaid income** is income which has been paid in an accounting period but relates to the next accounting period, eg advance ticket sales revenue received by a theatre.

The next 8 pages explain in full the accounting treatment of accruals and payments.

# accrued expense

## what is it?

An accrued expense is an expense that belongs to an accounting period but which has not been paid at the end of that period.

### how is it dealt with in the accounts?

- an estimate of the amount of the expense, or the actual expense if known, is added to the expense account at the end of the period for inclusion in the statement of profit or loss
- the amount is shown in the statement of financial position as a current liability

### what are the accounting entries?

- **debit** the expense account with the accrued amount
- **credit** the expense account with the total to be transferred to the statement of profit or loss
- bring down a **credit** balance in the expense account in the new period – this will reduce the amount of the expense in the new period when the bill is paid

Now study the example shown below.

## EXAMPLE of an accrued expense

A £500 power bill for electricity is received in January for the previous year ending 31 December.

The expense accrued is shown in the Light and heat account shown below.

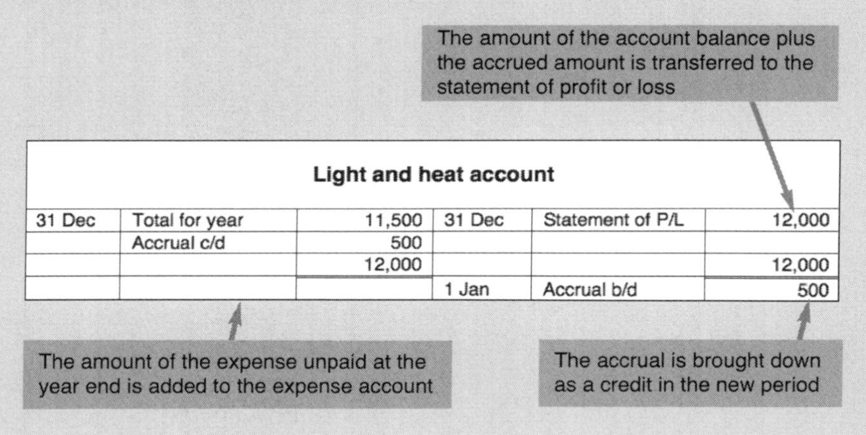


**Light and heat account**

| | | | | | |
|---|---|---|---|---|---|
| 31 Dec | Total for year | 11,500 | 31 Dec | Statement of P/L | 12,000 |
| | Accrual c/d | 500 | | | |
| | | 12,000 | | | 12,000 |
| | | | 1 Jan | Accrual b/d | 500 |

# accrued income

## what is it?

Accrued income is income that belongs to an accounting period but which has not been received at the end of that period.

### how is it dealt with in the accounts?

- an estimate of the amount of income, or the actual income if known, is added to the income account at the end of the period for inclusion in the statement of profit or loss
- the amount is shown in the statement of financial position as a current asset

### what are the accounting entries?

- **credit** the income account with the accrued amount
- **debit** the income account with the total to be transferred to the statement of profit or loss
- bring down a **debit** balance in the income account in the new period – this will reduce the amount of the income in the new period when the amount is received

Now study the example shown below.

## EXAMPLE of accrued income

£1,500 commission is due for the year ending 31 December. It is received in January.

The income accrued is shown in the Commission receivable account.

The amount of the account balance plus the accrued amount is transferred to the statement of profit or loss

| Commission receivable account | | | | | |
|---|---|---|---|---|---|
| 31 Dec | Statement of P/L | 10,000 | 31 Dec | Total for the year | 8,500 |
| | | | | Accrual c/d | 1,500 |
| | | 10,000 | | | 10,000 |
| 1 Jan | Accrual b/d | 1,500 | | | |

The accrual is brought down as a debit in the new period

The amount of the income unpaid at the year end is added to the income account

# prepaid expense

## what is it?

A prepaid expense that has been paid in advance during one accounting period but belongs to the next period.

### how is it dealt with in the accounts?

- the amount of the advance payment is deducted from the balance of the expense account at the end of the period; the amount for inclusion in the statement of profit or loss is the total paid in the period less the prepayment
- the amount of the prepayment is shown in the statement of financial position as a current asset

### what are the accounting entries?

- **credit** the expense account with the accrued amount
- **credit** the expense account with the total to be transferred to the statement of profit or loss
- bring down a **debit** balance in the expense account in the new period – this will reduce the amount of the expense in the new period to which it belongs

Now study the example shown below.

## EXAMPLE of a prepaid expense

£750 rent has been paid in December for the month of January the following year. The year end is 31 December.

The amount of the prepayment is shown in the Rent paid account.

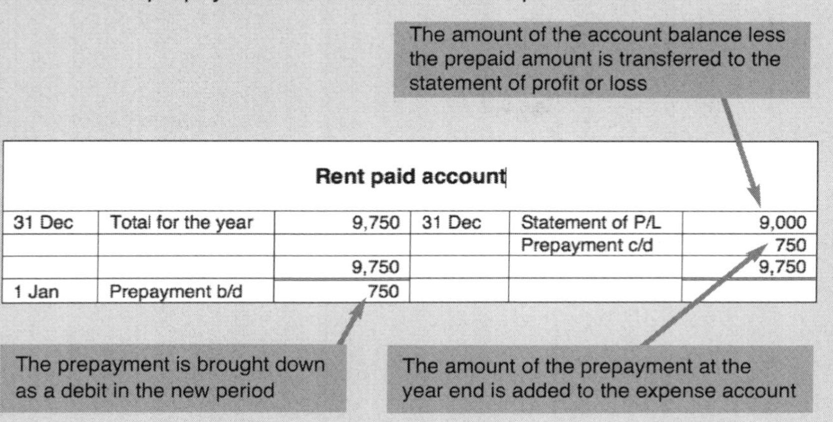


**Rent paid account**

| | | | | | |
|---|---|---|---|---|---|
| 31 Dec | Total for the year | 9,750 | 31 Dec | Statement of P/L | 9,000 |
| | | | | Prepayment c/d | 750 |
| | | 9,750 | | | 9,750 |
| 1 Jan | Prepayment b/d | 750 | | | |

## prepaid income

### what is it?

Prepaid income is income that has been received in advance during one accounting period but belongs to the next period.

### how is it dealt with in the accounts?

- the amount of the advance payment is deducted from the balance of the income account at the end of the period; the amount for inclusion in the statement of profit or loss is the total received in the period less the prepayment
- the amount of the prepayment is shown in the statement of financial position as a current liability

### what are the accounting entries?

- **debit** the income account with the prepaid amount
- **debit** the income account with the total to be transferred to the statement of profit or loss
- bring down a **credit** balance in the expense account in the new period – this will increase the amount of the expense in the new period to which it belongs

Now study the example shown below.

## EXAMPLE of prepaid income

£5,000 has been received for theatre ticket sales during the year ending 31 December which relate to performances in the following financial year.

The income prepaid is shown in the Ticket sales account.

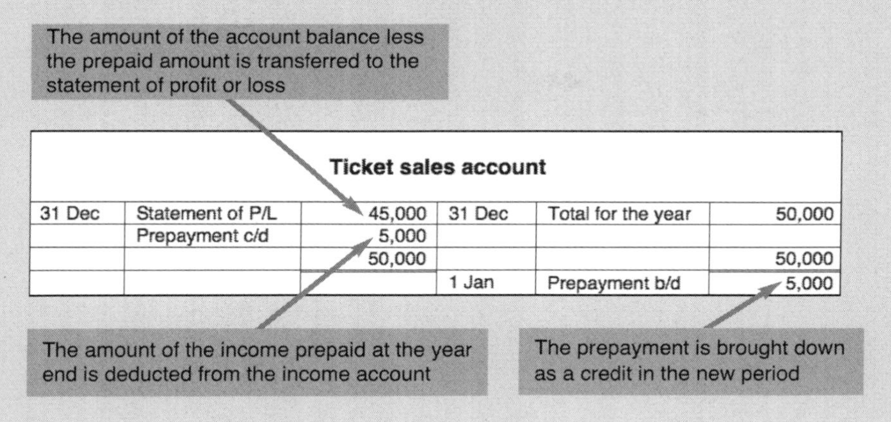


**Ticket sales account**

| | | | | | |
|---|---|---|---|---|---|
| 31 Dec | Statement of P/L | 45,000 | 31 Dec | Total for the year | 50,000 |
| | Prepayment c/d | 5,000 | | | |
| | | 50,000 | | | 50,000 |
| | | | 1 Jan | Prepayment b/d | 5,000 |

## accounting entries from previous periods

Expense and income accounts that include accruals and prepayments often feature them in consecutive financial periods. So you may have to deal with values accrued or prepaid at the beginning of a period from the **previous period**, and new accruals and prepayments to enter for the **end of the current period**, as in the following examples:

**EXAMPLE**

The Light and heat account has opened the current year with an expense accrued from the previous year; this will show as a **credit**, reducing the expense in the current year and being paid during the year.

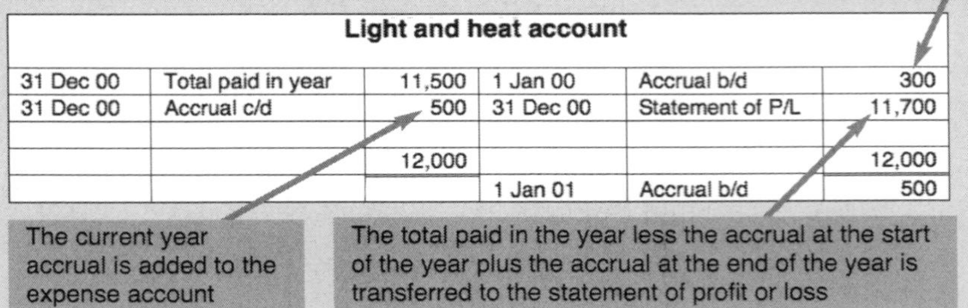


| Light and heat account | | | | | |
|---|---|---|---|---|---|
| 31 Dec 00 | Total paid in year | 11,500 | 1 Jan 00 | Accrual b/d | 300 |
| 31 Dec 00 | Accrual c/d | 500 | 31 Dec 00 | Statement of P/L | 11,700 |
| | | | | | |
| | | 12,000 | | | 12,000 |
| | | | 1 Jan 01 | Accrual b/d | 500 |

In some circumstances an account may start the year with a prepayment and end it with an accrual, or vice versa.

**EXAMPLE**

The Rent paid account may have opened the current year with a prepayment from the previous year. This would show as a **debit**, adding to the expense in the current year.

The prepaid rent belonging to the previous year is brought down as a debit in the current year (00)

**Rent paid account**

| | | | | | |
|---|---|---|---|---|---|
| 1 Jan 00 | Prepayment b/d | 750 | 31 Dec 00 | Statement of P/L | 9,000 |
| 31 Dec 00 | Total paid in year | 7,750 | | | |
| 31 Dec 00 | Accrual c/d | 500 | | | |
| | | | | | |
| | | 9,000 | | | 9,000 |
| | | | 1 Jan 01 | Accrual b/d | 500 |

The current year accrual is added to the expense account

The total paid in the year plus the prepayment at the start of the year plus the accrual at the end of the year is transferred to the statement of profit or loss

## 'pro-rata' prepayments

'Pro-rata' means 'a proportion of'. So if a full-time job offers an annual salary of £30,000, and you do the job part-time, eg 50% of the hours, your salary will be a 'pro-rata' 50% of £30,000, ie £15,000. As accruals and prepayments can often overlap different accounting periods – eg financial years – you will end up having to calculate **a proportion of the full amount to allocate to the individual periods**.

For example, a business with an accounting year end of 31 December might pay an insurance premium for 12 months starting 1 August, or it might pay rent in advance for the 3 months December to February. In both these cases the business must calculate the 'pro-rata' proportion of the value relating to the part of each year. The calculations are as follows:

**Example 1:**
An insurance premium of £1,200 is paid on 1 August 00 for the 12 months ending 31 July 01.

**Solution**:
January-July 01 is prepaid expense. Enter a prepayment for 7/12ths of £1,200 = £700.

**Example 2:**
Rent of £9,000 is paid on 1 December 00 for the quarter ending 28 February 01.

**Solution:**
January and February 01 is a prepaid expense. Enter a prepayment for 2/3rds of £9,000 = £6,000.

## 'pro-rata' income receipts

Income receipts may also overlap different accounting periods.

Here are some examples:

**Example 1:**

Income in the form of tuition fees of £2,000 is received in October 00.

The income covers the 4 month period November 00 to February 01.

The year end is 31 December.

**Solution**:
The two months January and February 01 are in the next period and so represent **prepaid income.**

Enter a prepayment for **2/4ths** of £2,000 = £1,000

**Example 2:**

Income in the form of licence fees of £4,800 is received in November 00.

The fees cover the one year period from December 00 to November 01.

The year end is 31 December.

**Solution:**
The 11 months January to November 01 are in the next period and so represent **prepaid income**.

Enter a prepayment for **11/12ths** of £4,800 = £4,400

# 5 Depreciation

## *SPREADING THE COST OF NON-CURRENT ASSETS*

*The cost of a non-current asset is spread over the amount of time that the asset is expected to be of use to the business. A proportion of the total cost is charged to the accounts in each financial period. This reflects the accruals principle. Depreciation is the method used to calculate this cost.*

## external and internal guidelines for calculating depreciation

**International Accounting Standard 16 (IAS 16) – external guidelines**

This states how non-current assets should be accounted for and defines depreciation as

'the systematic allocation of the cost of an asset less its residual value over its useful life'

**internal guidelines (business policy) for methods of depreciation**

- straight line
- straight line with residual value
- straight line pro-rata part year
- diminishing balance

The annual depreciation rate can be:

- a percentage of original cost (eg 20%)
- a fraction of original cost (eg 1/5)

## International Accounting Standard 16 (IAS 16)

IAS 16, sets out the accounting treatment of non-current assets, referring to them collectively as **property, plant and equipment**.

Elements of the depreciation process are defined by IAS 16 as follows:

| | |
|---|---|
| **useful life** | The period of time over which the asset is expected to be used. |
| **residual value** | The amount the business expects to be able to sell the asset for when it is no longer of use to the business. |
| **depreciable amount** | The total cost of an asset less any residual value. |
| **carrying amount** | The value of an asset shown in the statement of financial position after deducting accumulated depreciation. Also referred to as "net book value". |

IAS 16 states that depreciation must be charged on all non-current assets except on freehold land. It describes methods of depreciation including **straight line** and **diminishing balance** (also known as **reducing balance**).

## depreciation methods explained

### straight line method

An equal amount for reduction in value of the asset is charged in each period, so that at the end of the useful life of the asset it will have a zero value.

**EXAMPLE**

A machine cost £10,000 and is estimated to have a useful life of 5 years.

So 20%, or 1/5th, of the value (£2,000) will be charged as depreciation to the statement of profit or loss each year. At the end of the final year it will have no value.

| | |
|---|---|
| Year 1 | £2,000 |
| Year 2 | £2,000 |
| Year 3 | £2,000 |
| Year 4 | £2,000 |
| Year 5 | £2,000 |

**straight line with residual value method of depreciation**

The amount to be charged over the life of the asset is

*original cost of the asset minus any estimated residual value*

'Residual value' is the value left in the asset when it is disposed of.

This is called 'scrap value'.

**EXAMPLE**

A machine cost £10,000 and is estimated to have a useful life of 5 years and a residual scrap value of £2,000.

The depreciable amount is £8,000 (£10,000 – £2,000), so the annual depreciation is £1,600 (£8,000 x 20%).

| | |
|---|---|
| Year 1 | £1,600 |
| Year 2 | £1,600 |
| Year 3 | £1,600 |
| Year 4 | £1,600 |
| Year 5 | £1,600 |

£2,000 scrap value after 5 years

### straight line method 'pro-rata' part year

This is the situation where it is business policy to charge straight line depreciation over the life of the asset for **periods of less than a year**, eg a period of months.

**EXAMPLE**

A machine cost £10,000 and is estimated to have a useful life of 5 years. It was purchased half way through a financial year and so depreciation is charged every six months.

£2,000 will be charged to the statement of profit or loss each year except in the year of acquisition and the year of disposal when only a part year (6 months) charge is made:

6 months' depreciation
= £1,000
(ie £2,000 ÷ 6/12)

4 years' depreciation
= £2,000 x 4
= £8,000

6 months' depreciation
= £1,000
(ie £2,000 ÷ 2)

**diminishing balance method (also known as 'reducing balance' method)**

A fixed percentage is charged in each period based on the original cost less depreciation to date. As a result a higher amount of depreciation is charged in the early years and the amount gets smaller (diminishes) every year. The asset value will therefore never reach zero.

**EXAMPLE**

A delivery van costing £30,000 is depreciated by the diminishing balance method at 25% per year. A lesser amount is charged each year:

| | | |
|---|---|---|
| Year 1 | £7,500 | (£30,000 x 25%) |
| Year 2 | £5,625 | (£22,500 [£30,000 - £7,500] x 25%) |
| Year 3 | £4,219 | (£16,875 x 25%) |
| Year 4 | £3,164 | (£12,656 x 25%) |
| Year 5 | £2,373 | (£9,492 x 25%) |

The original cost of the asset is never written off so a residual value figure is not applicable in diminishing (reducing) balance depreciation.

## accounting entries for depreciation

The depreciation charge for a period is **debited** to Depreciation expense account and **credited** to Accumulated depreciation account

**EXAMPLE**

The machine costing £10,000 is estimated to have a useful life of 5 years and is depreciated by the straight line method.

**Accounting entries Year 1:**

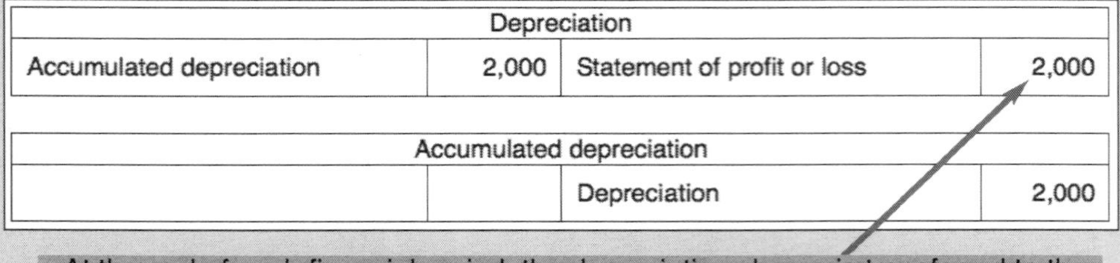

| Depreciation | | | |
|---|---|---|---|
| Accumulated depreciation | 2,000 | Statement of profit or loss | 2,000 |

| Accumulated depreciation | | | |
|---|---|---|---|
| | | Depreciation | 2,000 |

At the end of each financial period, the depreciation charge is transferred to the statement of profit or loss. The Depreciation account returns to zero balance.

**But what happens to the account showing the original cost of the asset?**
**Answer:** it is unchanged by the entries for depreciation.

**Accounting entries for Years 1 and 2 depreciation:**

| Depreciation | | | |
|---|---|---|---|
| Accumulated depreciation (Year 1) | 2,000 | Statement of profit or loss (Year 1) | 2,000 |
| Accumulated depreciation (Year 2) | 2,000 | Statement of profit or loss (Year 2) | 2,000 |

| Accumulated depreciation – machinery | | | |
|---|---|---|---|
| Balance c/d (Year 1) | 2,000 | Depreciation (Year 1) | 2,000 |
| Balance c/d (Year 2) | 4,000 | Balance b/d (Year 2) | 2,000 |
| | | Depreciation (Year 2) | 2,000 |
| | 4,000 | | 4,000 |
| | | Balance b/d | 4,000 |

Each period's depreciation builds up in the Accumulated depreciation account until the asset has reached zero value **carrying amount**, or until it is disposed of.

**Note:** The **carrying amount** is calculated by taking the original cost and subtracting the accumulated depreciation.

# 6 Irrecoverable and doubtful debts

## *DEALING WITH ACCOUNTS THAT HAVE GONE 'BAD'*

*Customer account balances (debits) are a valuable asset of a business. But if it becomes clear that an account will never be repaid, perhaps because the customer is bankrupt or in liquidation, then this amount has become '**irrecoverable**' and must be written off in the sales ledger and treated as an expense. Businesses must also regularly review customer accounts that may become irrecoverable; these are '**doubtful**' debts.*

## journals for writing off irrecoverable debts

- **VAT-registered businesses – the account entries:**

  Debit Irrecoverable debts

  Debit VAT

  Credit Sales ledger control and customer account in the sales ledger

  **Note:** the total value of the amount owed is transferred from the Sales ledger control account but split between VAT and Irrecoverable debts.

- **businesses that are not VAT-registered – the account entries:**

  Debit Irrecoverable debts

  Credit Sales ledger control and customer account in the sales ledger

  **Note:** the total value of the amount owed is transferred from the Sales ledger control account to Irrecoverable debts.

**What if a debt written off in a previous period as irrecoverable is then paid?**

The account entries will be:

Debit Bank

Credit Debts recovered (or Irrecoverable debts account)

## debts that become doubtful debts

It is acceptable practice to estimate the cost of **future** irrecoverable debts. This is done by creating an **allowance for doubtful debts** which may be either a specific value or a percentage of the total value of trade receivables. The amount of this allowance is likely to be influenced by previous experience of the level of debts that become irrecoverable.

## allowance for doubtful debts – double entry

Note the effects in each case on both the statement of profit or loss and the statement of financial position.

| Allowance | Debit | Credit |
| --- | --- | --- |
| **Creating an allowance for the first time** | Allowance for doubtful debts adjustment (SPL) | Allowance for doubtful debts (SFP) |
| **Increasing the allowance in a subsequent period** | Allowance for doubtful debts adjustment (SPL) | Allowance for doubtful debts (SFP) |
| **Decreasing the allowance in a subsequent period** | Allowance for doubtful debts (SFP) | Allowance for doubtful debts adjustment (SPL) |

## what the financial statements show

- **Statement of profit or loss**: the Allowance for doubtful debts adjustment account takes care of any annual **changes to the allowance**, up (debit) or down (credit).
- **Statement of financial position**: the Allowance for doubtful debts account shows **the actual level of allowance** each year – and fluctuations in the level year by year.

**EXAMPLE**

**Year 1:** Trade receivables are £100,000. It is expected that 2% of these debts will not be paid. An allowance for doubtful debts of £2,000 is created. This will be shown as an expense in the statement of profit or loss. The entries are as follows:

Allowance for doubtful debts adjustment (SPL)

| Debit | Credit |
|---|---|
| 2,000 | |

Allowance for doubtful debts (SFP)

| Debit | Credit |
|---|---|
| | 2,000 |

**Year 2:** Trade receivables are £80,000. A 2% allowance is still required but the amount is now reduced to £1,600 and so a downwards adjustment of £400 is made. This will be shown as income in the statement of profit or loss. The entries are:

Allowance for doubtful debts adjustment (SPL)

| Debit | Credit |
|---|---|
| | 400 |

Allowance for doubtful debts (SFP)

| | Debit | | Credit |
|---|---|---|---|
| Bal c/d | 2,000 | | 2,000 |
| Adj (SPL) | 400 | Bal b/d | 2,000 |
| Bal c/d | 1,600 | | |
| | 2,000 | | 2,000 |
| | | Bal b/d | 1,600 |

**Note:**

- there is no VAT element in the doubtful debts allowance
- there is no need to amend the doubtful debts allowance for any irrecoverable debts incurred

# 7 Accounting Standards and concepts

## *THE NEED FOR RULES AND GUIDELINES*

*Accounting practice is based on agreed rules and guidelines, adopted by all those involved in keeping accounting records and drawing up financial statements. As a result of these rules and guidelines the financial statements of businesses are prepared in a way that provides uniformity and comparability and ensures that they are easily understood by users.*

## rules and guidelines you will need to know

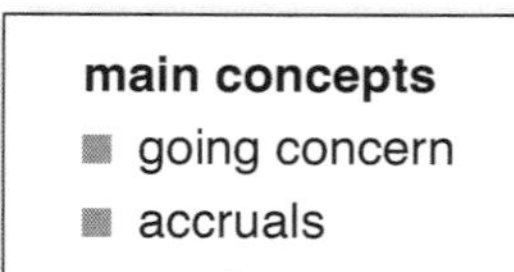


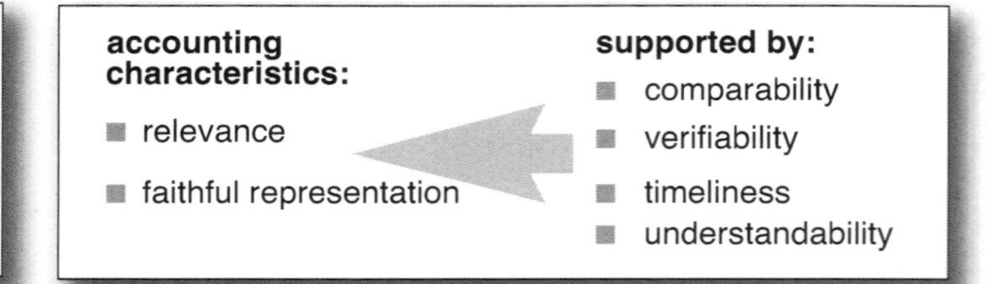

## Accounting Standards

Accounting practice complies with published accounting standards, both in the UK and worldwide.

The particular standards relevant to this AAT unit are:

- **IAS 16 Property, plant and equipment**

  This sets out the accounting treatment for non-current assets, including depreciation. (See Chapter 5 page 39).

- **IAS 2 Inventories**

  This covers the methods of valuation of inventory.

  (See Chapter 8, page 58).

# concepts explained

## going concern

This concept assumes that the business will continue to trade in the foreseeable future.

The value of the assets of a business that is not continuing to trade (a 'gone concern') may be different to those of a going concern.

**EXAMPLE**
Machinery which has value in the working factory of a going concern is likely to become almost valueless when the business ceases to trade.

## accruals

Income and expenses must be matched.

The income in the statement of profit or loss is the income **earned** in that accounting period.

The expenses in the statement of profit or loss are the expenses incurred in **earning the income** of the period, but may not necessarily be paid for in that period.

**EXAMPLE**

Sales made and invoiced in the last month of a financial year will be recorded for that year even though they may not be paid for until the next year.

## consistency

Accounting methods and presentation should be applied consistently from one financial period to another.

**EXAMPLES**

- If inventory is valued using FIFO, it should continue to be valued using FIFO.
- If vehicles are depreciated at 25%, diminishing balance method, that is how they will continue to be depreciated every year.

## prudence

If there is any uncertainty about a value, financial statements should report a conservative or cautious figure. Recent developments in accounting have used the word 'neutral' rather than prudent.

This concept ensures that values are not misstated in such a way that they could distort profits or misrepresent values in the statement of financial position.

**EXAMPLES**

- Valuation of inventory at the lower of cost and net realisable value.
- Inclusion of an allowance for doubtful debt.

## accounting characteristics explained

### relevance

Information reported should be useful to its users.

This characteristic includes the concept of **materiality**, which recognises that some rules relating to the preparation of financial statements need not apply to very low-value items.

**EXAMPLES**

- Grouping of small miscellaneous expenses in a sundry expense account.
- Low-value permanent assets, such as staplers or calculators, need not be treated as non-current assets.

### faithful representation

Information should reliable and can be depended upon.

Information is truthful, accurate and free from error or bias.

**EXAMPLE**

Inventory values in the financial statements are correct and based on consistently applied valuation methods.

The accounting characteristics of relevance and faithful representation are supported by the characteristics of **comparability**, **verifiability**, **timeliness** and **understandability**:

**comparability**

Users can compare the current information with that of previous periods or other businesses. This allows users to draw conclusions about performance and financial health of a business.

**verifiability**

The accuracy of the information can be verified.

**timeliness**

Information must be available in time for decisions to be based on it.

**understandability**

The information is presented clearly so that users can understand it.

## examples of accounting principles in action

The examples on the next two pages show how accounting principles are reflected in accounting entries and period-end adjustments.

| Entry/Adjustment | Relevant principle/concept plus an explanation |
| --- | --- |
| Insurance prepaid at the period end | **Accruals**. Only the part of the payment that belongs to the current period should be included as an expense. |
| Depreciation of non-current assets | **Accruals**. The cost of the non-current asset is spread over the number of years it is expected to have a useful life within the business. |
| Allowance for doubtful debts | **Prudence**. The value of receivables should not be overstated because some debts may not be repaid.<br>**Accruals**. The expense of the unpaid debt should be matched to the period in which it is incurred. |
| Entry of closing inventory value at net realisable value | **Prudence.** The original cost of the inventory will not be realised so the likely sale value (net realisable value) is used. |

| | |
|---|---|
| ■ Purchase of desk lamp for £35 | **Relevance/materiality**. Although the lamp may last for several years, its value does not warrant it being treated as a non-current asset. |
| ■ Value of goods sold but not yet paid for at the year-end | **Accruals**. Income is recognised in the period in which it is earned. |
| ■ Furniture and fittings depreciated by the same method and percentage in each period | **Consistency**. Unless there is a sound reason for changing (which would be noted in the financial statements), the same percentage and method should be applied.<br>**Going concern**. The rate of depreciation assumes that the business will continue to trade in the foreseeable future. |

# 8 Inventories

## *THE NEED TO VALUE INVENTORY*

*Businesses that keep inventory must know the value of that inventory in order to produce accurate financial statements. Inventory is normally valued at the end of a financial period and included in both the statement of profit and loss and also in the statement of financial position. Methods of valuing inventory are set out in IAS 2.*

### IAS 2 – the principle of valuation

*Inventory is valued at the lower of cost and net realisable value.*

**Cost** = original purchase cost. **Net realisable value (NRV)** = the estimated selling price less the estimated costs incurred in getting the product to saleable condition.

### IAS 2 – methods of valuation

- **FIFO**: First in, First out
- **AVCO**: Weighted average cost

*Note that* **LIFO** *(Last in, First out) is a method that may be used for internal purposes but is not covered by IAS 2 and cannot be used to produce financial statements.*

## accounting entries for inventory

If inventory is held at the beginning of a financial period, it will be in the accounting records as a debit in the Inventory account. This figure is also the closing inventory at the end of the previous period. It will have remained unchanged throughout the current period. This is the **opening inventory**.

At the end of the period a new inventory value will be established because the inventory level is most likely to have changed during the period. This is **closing inventory**.

The accounting entries for inventory at the end of the financial period are:

| **Opening inventory value:** | | **Closing inventory value:** | |
|---|---|---|---|
| Dr | Statement of profit or loss (Cost of sales section) | Dr | Inventory |
| Cr | Inventory | Cr | Statement of profit or loss (Cost of sales section) |

Both the opening and closing inventory values are used in the calculation of Cost of sales in the statement of profit or loss to show the change in the value of inventory.

See the example on the next page.

**EXAMPLE – calculating cost of sales**

| | |
|---|---|
| Opening inventory at the beginning of the period | £53,000 |
| Purchases during the period | £318,000 |
| Closing inventory valued at the end of the period | £48,000 |

The Cost of sales (or Cost of goods sold) is calculated as:

*inventory value at the start of the period* ***plus*** *the cost of inventory purchased during the period* ***less*** *the value of inventory left at the end of the period:*

| | | |
|---|---|---|
| | Opening inventory | 53,000 |
| *plus* | Purchases | 318,000 |
| *less* | Closing inventory | (48,000) |
| *equals* | Cost of sales | 323,000 |

**What can and what cannot be included in the cost of inventory?**

| | |
|---|---|
| purchase cost ✔ | storage costs ✕ |
| delivery cost ✔ | selling costs ✕ |
| conversion costs ✔ | |

# methods of inventory valuation

## inventory valuation – principles and policy

- If the purchase price of inventory items remains the same, methods of valuation make no difference to the inventory valuation.

  But if prices fluctuate, the different methods of valuation give different valuation totals.

- Methods of valuation do not necessarily reflect the actual movement of inventory – ie what inventory goes in or out of the business – they are simply principles by which inventories are valued for accounting purposes.

- Business policy will state which method is to be adopted for valuing inventory and this method cannot be changed.

  So it is not possible for inventory valuation methods to change from one year to the next in order to show an increase (or decrease) in the profitability of the business in the statement of profit or loss.

## inventory valuation – FIFO (First in, First out)

- The principle of valuation is that **the oldest inventory is issued first**.
- Remaining inventory is therefore valued at **more recent prices**.
- Remember that this does **not** mean that all the old inventory is got rid of first – it may be that old inventory sits around for much longer than newer inventory.

  FIFO is only **a method of valuation** which must be applied consistently.

**EXAMPLE OF FIFO**

Week 1 — 10 desks are received into the warehouse at a cost of £100 per desk. The total value of the desks received is £1,000 (ie 10 x £100).

Week 2 — A further 10 desks are received at a cost of £80 per desk. The total value of these desks is £800 (ie 10 x £80).

Week 3 — 7 desks are sold and taken out of the warehouse. These are costed at £100 per desk (oldest inventory) = total value £700. 13 desks remain.

**Closing inventory (inventory left**) is 3 x £100 (the oldest inventory) + 10 x £80 (the next lot of inventory received)

= £300 (Week 1) + £800 (Week 2) = **£1,100**

## inventory valuation – AVCO (AVerage COst)

- The principle of valuation is that after each receipt or issue of inventory, **the remaining inventory is re-valued at weighted average cost**.

**EXAMPLE OF AVCO**

Week 1 10 desks are received at a cost of £100 per desk = total value £1,000.

Week 2 A further 10 desks are received at a cost of £80 per desk. The total value of these desks is £800 (ie 10 x £80).

Inventory is now 20 desks at a weighted average cost of £90 per desk, calculated as follows:

$$\frac{\text{£1,000 (cost of first 10 desks) + £800 (cost of next 10 desks)}}{\text{20 (number of desks now in inventory)}} = \textbf{£90}$$

Week 3 7 desks are sold and taken out of the warehouse. These are costed at £90 per desk (weighted average) = total value £630.

**Closing inventory (inventory left**) is 13 desks valued at:

13 x £90 (the weighted average) = **£1,170**

## inventory valuation – LIFO (Last in, First out)

- LIFO is **not recognised under IAS 2** and so cannot be used as a basis for drawing up the statement of profit or loss, or the statement of financial position, **unless** it is for internal information for the business.
- The principle of **valuation** is that the **newest inventory is issued first**. Remaining inventory is therefore valued at oldest prices.

**EXAMPLE OF LIFO**

Week 1 — 10 desks are received at a cost of £100 per desk = total value £1,000.

Week 2 — A further 10 desks are received at a cost of £80 per desk. The total value of these desks is £800 (ie 10 x £80).

Week 3 — 7 desks are sold and taken out of the warehouse. These are costed at £80 per desk (the newest inventory received)
= total value £560 (ie 7 x £80)

**Closing inventory (inventory left)** is valued as follows:

| | | |
|---|---|---|
| 10 x £100 (the desks received in Week 1) | = | £1,000 |
| 3 x £80 (the desks received in Week 2) | = | £240 |
| Valuation | = | £1,240 |

## Summary of closing inventory values using FIFO, AVCO and LIFO

| FIFO = £1,100 | AVCO = £1,170 | LIFO = £1,240 |
|---|---|---|

## Effect of different valuations

- At a time of **falling prices** (as shown in the example), FIFO will give a **lower valuation** than other methods and therefore a lower profit since less value of closing stock is deducted in the Cost of sales calculation.
- At a time of **rising prices**, FIFO will give a **higher valuation** than other methods and therefore a higher profit since more value of closing stock is deducted in the Cost of sales calculation.
- At a time of falling prices, LIFO (if used for internal information) would give a higher valuation than other methods and therefore a higher profit since more value of closing stock is deducted in the Cost of sales calculation.
- At a time of rising prices, LIFO (if used for internal information) would give a lower valuation than other methods and therefore a lower profit since less value of closing stock is deducted in the Cost of Sales calculation.
- AVCO will simply give an 'average' valuation between LIFO and FIFO.

## margin or mark-up?

Inventory value (the cost of an item) and the selling price can be calculated if the **margin** or **mark-up** is known. What is the difference between margin and mark-up?

- **margin** = profit expressed as a percentage of sales
- **mark-up** = profit expressed as a percentage of cost

The two examples below show the difference between margin and mark-up applied to the same product:

**EXAMPLE – using margin to calculate the cost of an item**

What is the cost of a product that sells at £100 with a sales margin of 20%?

Answer: £100 less £20 margin (ie **20% of £100**) = £80

Note: the cost of £80 is 80% of the selling price of £100

**EXAMPLE – using mark-up to calculate the selling price of an item**

What is the selling price of a product that has a cost of £80 and a mark-up of 25%

Answer: £80 plus £20 mark-up (ie **25% of £80**) = £100

Note : the selling price of £100 is 125% of the cost of £80.

## calculating inventory value from margin and mark-up

We will now show how inventory value can be calculated from both margin and mark-up.

### calculation using margin

Process: 1 Calculate total inventory at selling price.

2 Deduct the margin on sales to arrive at inventory cost.

**EXAMPLE**

Inventory at selling price is £20,000; margin is 40%

Cost of inventory is: £20,000 less margin of £8,000 (ie 40% of £20,000) = £12,000

### calculation using mark-up

Process: 1 Calculate total inventory at selling price.

2 Deduct the mark-up to arrive at inventory cost.

**EXAMPLE**

Inventory at selling price is £20,000; mark-up is 25% (so selling price is 125% of cost)

Cost of inventory is: $\frac{20,000}{125} \times 100 = £16,000$

# 9 Acquisition of non-current assets

## *NON-CURRENT ASSETS*

*A reminder!*

***Non-current assets** are assets that are acquired for use within a business for the long term. 'Long term' normally means for more than one year.*

*The lists below set out the areas you will need to know when studying this subject.*

**categories of non-current asset**

- land and buildings
- motor vehicles
- plant and machinery
- furniture
- fixtures and fittings
- computers
- office equipment

**acquisition of non-current assets – questions to ask**

- what are the accounting entries?
- capital or revenue expenditure?
- what do you include in the value?
- what are the funding methods?
- what is the authorisation process for purchasing a non-current asset?

## acquisition of non-current assets – what are the accounting entries?

The cost of the non-current asset is **debited** to the asset account and **credited** to either the Bank account (if paid for immediately) or the supplier's account (if bought on credit). Any VAT charged on the non-current asset is **debited** to the VAT account. If the purchaser is not VAT-registered the total asset cost (including VAT) is **debited** to the asset account.

### EXAMPLE – accounting entries

A business purchases a new machine on 30 June. The machine costs £5,000 plus £1,000 VAT, a total of £6,000. It is paid for immediately by bank transfer; the entries are shown below. (Note that if the machine had been purchased on credit the credit entry would have been to the supplier's account and not to the Bank account).

| Plant and machinery | | | | | |
|---|---|---|---|---|---|
| 30 June | Bank | 5,000 | | | |

| VAT | | | | | |
|---|---|---|---|---|---|
| 30 June | Bank | 1,000 | | | |

| Bank | | | | | |
|---|---|---|---|---|---|
| | | | 30 June | Plant & machinery | 6,000 |

## acquisition of non-current assets – capital or revenue expenditure?

- **Capital expenditure**: *the purchase, alteration or improvement of non-current assets.* This includes the purchase price of an asset plus the cost of getting the asset to its location and into working condition.
- **Revenue expenditure**: *day-to-day running expenses, including looking after non-current assets.* This includes administration, selling, distribution and general overheads and also the repair, maintenance and servicing of non-current assets.

## non-current assets – dealing with capital and revenue costs

Separate the costs into capital and revenue items and post them to the relevant asset or expense accounts. See the two examples that follow.

**EXAMPLE 1 – invoiced amounts relating to new production machinery**

| Items | Treatment |
|---|---|
| Cost of machine<br>Delivery costs<br>Installation costs<br>Testing costs | **capital expenditure:**<br>add the items together and debit the asset account |
| Insurance costs<br>Consumables, eg oil | **revenue expenditure**:<br>debit the expense accounts |

**EXAMPLE 2 – the costs of building an extension to business premises**

| Items | Treatment |
|---|---|
| Site preparation<br>Building materials<br>Delivery cost of materials<br>Legal and professional fees<br>Builders' wages (own labour force) | **capital expenditure:** add the items together and debit the asset account |
| Building insurance<br>Repairs and redecoration of existing premises | **revenue expenditure**: debit expense accounts |

## when is an asset treated as an expense? . . . a note on capitalisation policy

If a non-current asset is defined as something that will last a business more than a year, then what about buying a waste bin, a kettle, a stapler or a calculator, all of which might be expected to give several years' service?

Businesses generally have a **capitalisation policy** which states a value below which an item is not capitalised (ie not treated as a non-current asset). In a small business, this value may be set at £100; larger businesses may set higher values.

**An item that costs less than the set value is treated as revenue expenditure** and debited to an expense account, eg an Office expenses account.

## financing non-current assets

Non-current assets are often high value items. A business may need to use **external funding** for acquiring the assets if the cash is not available within the business.

| | |
|---|---|
| **Borrowing** | A bank or finance company lends money in return for regular repayments plus interest. The money is paid into the business bank account and paid out again to the supplier of the asset. |
| **Hire purchase** | The business has use of the asset but a finance company owns it. A deposit and regular payments including interest are made to the finance company. Ownership of the asset usually passes to the business when all payments have been made. |
| **Finance lease** | The business has use of the asset but a finance company owns it. Regular payments including interest are made to the finance company. Ownership of the asset does not automatically pass to the business at the end of the agreement. |
| **Part-exchange** | An old asset is traded in against the new one at an agreed residual value. The balance outstanding is payable by cash (which may be borrowed). |

## authorisation process of non-current asset purchases

The purchase of non-current assets – often a major expenditure for a business – will be authorised by a senior person within the business:

- **small business**: this is likely to be the owner(s), ie a sole trader or the partners
- **larger organisation**: in a limited company, for example, there is likely to be a system for authorisation depending on the value of the asset being purchased: a departmental manager may authorise relatively low expenditure (say up to £5,000) or the approval of the Board of Directors may be needed for higher level expenditure

In a **larger organisation** the Policies and procedures documentation is likely to lay down the process for authorisation. This will usually include completion of a capital expenditure application form giving all relevant details of the expenditure including supplier quotation/s and reason for purchase.

Approval of the plan may depend on:

- availability of funding
- staff training requirements
- the extent to which the productivity or profitability of the business will be affected

# 10 Disposal of non-current assets

## *HOUSEKEEPING AND ACCOUNTING ON DISPOSAL*

*When a non-current asset is sold or scrapped, several accounting entries connected with that asset over its lifetime in the business are brought together in the disposal process.*

**the process deals with the following values:**

- original cost of the asset
- accumulated depreciation of the asset
- sale proceeds
- part-exchange value if relevant
- cost of replacement asset if part-exchange is involved

**accounts involved in the disposal process:**

- asset account (original cost)
- accumulated depreciation
- bank (if asset sold)
- disposal account

## disposal of non-current assets – accounting entries

These are the accounting entries for the sale of a non-current asset:

| | |
|---|---|
| **Debit** | Disposals account with original cost of the asset sold |
| **Credit** | Asset account with original cost of the asset sold |

| | |
|---|---|
| **Debit** | Accumulated depreciation account with accumulated depreciation of the asset sold |
| **Credit** | Disposals account with accumulated depreciation of the asset sold |

| | |
|---|---|
| **Debit** | Bank account with proceeds of sale |
| **Credit** | Disposals account with proceeds of sale |

A worked example is shown on the next page.

**EXAMPLE – disposal of a machine**

A business purchased a machine during the year ending 31 December 00 at a cost of £5,000. During the year ending 31 December 03 the machine is sold for £1,500 (scrap value). It has been depreciated on a straight line basis at 20%, ie £1,000. Depreciation is applied in the year of acquisition but not in the year of disposal. Accumulated depreciation is therefore £3,000 (3 years' depreciation) when the machine is sold. The Disposals account at 31 December 03 appears as follows:

| Disposals | | | | | |
|---|---|---|---|---|---|
| 31 Dec 03 | Machinery at cost | 5,000 | 31 Dec 03 | Accumulated Dep'n | 3,000 |
| | | | 31 Dec 03 | Bank | 1,500 |
| | | | 31 Dec 03 | Balance (loss) | 500 |
| | | 5,000 | | | 5,000 |

The balance of the Disposals account represents the profit or loss on the sale of the asset, the result of the sale proceeds not being exactly equal to the carrying amount of the asset at the time of sale. The profit or loss is shown in the statement of profit or loss as income (profit) or expense (loss).

Note that if there is no scrap value, there is no bank entry, but any loss will still be calculated as shown.

## disposal including part-exchange – accounting entries

Where an existing asset is used as part-payment for a replacement asset, the value given in part-exchange is entered in the Disposals account. The corresponding debit entry is entered in the non-current asset account at cost account.

**EXAMPLE – disposal of a machine including part-exchange**

A business purchased a machine during the year ending 31 December 00 at a cost of £5,000. Accumulated depreciation is £3,000. During the year ending 31 December 03 the machine is traded in for £2,250 against a new machine costing £10,000. The account entries are as follows:

| Disposals | | | | | |
|---|---|---|---|---|---|
| 31 Dec 03 | Machinery at cost | 5,000 | 31 Dec 03 | Accumulated Dep'n | 3,000 |
| 31 Dec 03 | Balance (profit) | 250 | 31 Dec 03 | Machinery at cost | 2,250 |
| | | 5,250 | | | 5,250 |

| Machinery at cost | | | | | |
|---|---|---|---|---|---|
| 31 Dec 00 | Bank | 5,000 | 31 Dec 03 | Disposals | 5,000 |
| 31 Dec 03 | Disposals (part-ex) | 2,250 | 31 Dec 03 | Balance | 10,000 |
| 31 Dec 03 | Bank | 7,750 | | | |
| | | 10,000 | | | 10,000 |

## asset register

**An asset register is a group of records of non-current assets held by a business.**

- It is used for internal control to record and track details of the individual assets over their life within a business. It is not part of double-entry. Entries are made when the asset is purchased, when depreciation is calculated and on disposal.
- In the asset register there is an entry for each individual asset whereas in the accounting system several assets may be grouped together in one account, eg vehicles.
- The asset register includes the following details of each asset:
  - description including serial number
  - date of acquisition
  - original cost (capital items only)
  - funding method (cash, part-exchange, loan, lease)
  - method and rate of depreciation
  - depreciation charge for each period
  - carrying amount
  - disposal proceeds (on disposal)
  - disposal date (on disposal)

**EXAMPLE – extract from an asset register**

A delivery van, registration RS10 NPU, was purchased on 30 June 20X0 for £16,000. It was bought on a finance lease. It has been depreciated at a rate of 25% diminishing balance. Depreciation is charged in the year of acquisition but not in the year of disposal. It was sold on 15 September 20X4 for £5,000.

Set out below are the entries that would appear in the asset register. If it has been kept up to date, then they will correspond to physical assets held. The assets should be checked periodically against the register and any discrepancies investigated.

| *Description/ serial no.* | *Acquis-ition date* | *Cost £* | *Dep'n charges* | *Carrying amount* | *Funding method* | *Disposal proceeds* | *Disposal date* |
|---|---|---|---|---|---|---|---|
| **Vehicles** | | | | | | | |
| RS10 NPU | 30/06/X0 | 16,000 | | | Lease | | |
| Year-end 31/12/X0 | | | 4,000.00 | 12,000.00 | | | |
| Year-end 31/12/X1 | | | 3,000.00 | 9,000.00 | | | |
| Year-end 31/12/X2 | | | 2,250.00 | 6,750.00 | | | |
| Year-end 31/12/X3 | | | 1,687.50 | 5,062.50 | | | |
| Year-end 31/12/X4 | | | 0.00 | 0.00 | | 5,000.00 | 15/09/X4 |

# 11 Control accounts

## *KEEPING CONTROL OF THE ACCOUNTS*

*A control account is a summary account, used to record periodically the totals of types of transaction recorded in a group of subsidiary accounts.*

*Control account totals are useful for management who need to monitor levels of customer debt, the total of payments due to credit suppliers or the amount of VAT due to HMRC.*

### points to remember about control accounts

- the main control accounts are the Sales ledger control account, the Purchase ledger control account and the VAT control account
- the balance of each control account should always equal the **total of the balances** of the subsidiary accounts

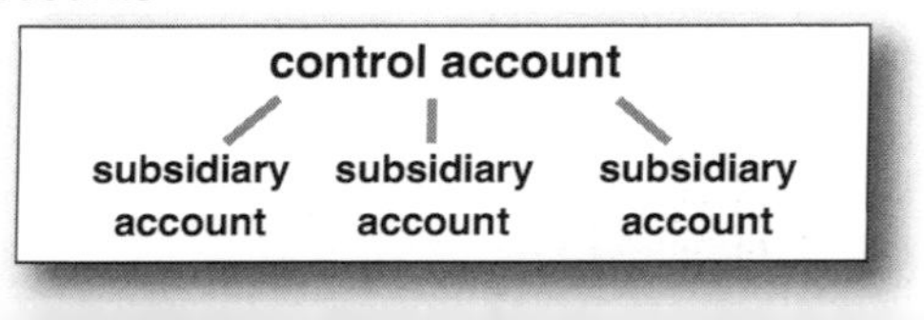

- the balance of each control account should be regularly **reconciled** with the total of the balances of the subsidiary accounts
- control accounts are useful in picking up errors in double-entry (see below)

**errors detected by the use of control accounts**

If double-entry has been completed correctly, the total of the subsidiary ledger account balances should be the same as the balance of the control account. Periodic checks in the form of reconciliations of these two totals are used to highlight errors. Examples of these are shown below.

**EXAMPLES – errors picked up by control account reconciliation**

- an irrecoverable debt written off in the customer account in the sales ledger but not entered in the Sales ledger control account
- discount received entered in the Purchases ledger control account but not entered in the supplier account in the purchases ledger
- a returned (dishonoured) customer cheque entered in the cash book but not entered in the customer account in the sales ledger

The main control accounts are illustrated and explained on the pages that follow.

## Sales ledger control account

The individual entries that make up the totals in the Sales ledger control account (SLCA) are to be found in the individual customer accounts in the sales ledger.

The balances at A and B should match the total of the opening (A) and closing (B) balances of individual customer accounts in the sales ledger.

| Sales ledger control | | | |
|---|---|---|---|
| Balance b/d A | X | Receipts from customers | X |
| Credit sales | X | Settlement discount allowed | X |
| Returned cheques | X | Sales returns | X |
| | | Irrecoverable debts | X |
| | | Set-off/contra entries | X |
| | | Balance c/d | X |
| | X | | X |
| Balance b/d B | X | | |

The corresponding (opposite) entry of the set-off/contra is contained in the Purchases ledger control account

## Sales ledger control account entries and sources

| *Entry* | *Dr/Cr* | *Value is:* | *Source* |
|---|---|---|---|
| Balance b/d | Dr | Total amount owing from customers at the beginning of the period | Balance c/d from previous period |
| Credit sales | Dr | Total amount (including VAT) invoiced to customers during the period | From 'total' column, Sales day book |
| Returned cheques | Dr | Value of any bounced cheques | From cash book |
| Receipts from customers | Cr | Total value of money received from customers during the period | From cash book - cash and bank columns |
| Settlement discount allowed | Cr | Total value of discount deducted by customers when paying | From cash book |
| Sales returns | Cr | Total value of credit notes (including VAT) issued to customers during the period | From 'total' column, Sales returns day book |
| Irrecoverable debts | Cr | Value of any customer balances that will not be paid | Journal |
| Set-off/ contra entry | Cr | Where a customer is also a supplier and amounts owing are set against each other in the ledgers | Journal |

**reconciliation of sales ledger control account and sales ledger**

If the double-entry has been completed correctly, the total of the subsidiary sales ledger account balances should agree with the balance of the Sales control account. These balances should be regularly **reconciled**. Possible reasons for discrepancies between the Sales ledger control account balance and the total of sales ledger balances could be caused by a number of errors:

**type of account entry**

- credit sales
- sales returns
- payments from customers
- settlement discount allowed
- irrecoverable debts
- set-off

**possible cause of account error**

- entry omitted
- entry understated ('undercast')
- entry made twice
- entry too high ('overcast')

Note: not all errors come to light in a reconciliation: there could be double-entry errors that require correction – for example, a transaction entered in the wrong subsidiary sales ledger account (error of commission) will not affect the balance reconciliation.

**EXAMPLE – sales ledger reconciliation: dealing with errors**

The sales ledger control account balance is £58,850 but the total of the customer account balances in the sales ledger is £54,529. The net difference of £4,321 is the result of the following three errors in the control account:

| **Errors in the Sales ledger control account** | **Difference** |
|---|---|
| 1. Set-off of £909 has been entered as £990 | £81 |
| 2. An irrecoverable debt for £48 has not been entered | £48 |
| 3. The sales returns book total of £2,177 has been entered on the wrong side of the control account | £4,354 |

Amendments needed in the Sales ledger control account are as follows:

| Sales ledger control | | | |
|---|---|---|---|
| Balance b/d | 58,850 | **2.** Irrecoverable debt | 48 |
| **1.** Set-off | 81 | **3.** Sales returns | 4,354 |
| Balance c/d | | Balance c/d | 54,529 |
| | 58,931 | | 58,931 |
| Balance b/d | 54,529 | | |

**58,850 + 81 – 48 – 4,354 = 54,529**

Note: this example shows errors in the control account. Any errors in the sales ledger accounts (eg settlement discount applied to the wrong customer) must be corrected by entries within the ledger accounts and not in the control account.

## Purchases ledger control account (PLCA)

The individual entries that make up the totals in the Purchases ledger control account (PLCA) are to be found in the individual supplier accounts in the purchases ledger.

The balances at C and D should match the total of the opening (C) and closing (D) balances of the individual supplier accounts in the purchases ledger.

| Purchases ledger control | | | |
|---|---|---|---|
| Payments to suppliers | X | Balance b/d C | X |
| Settlement discount received | X | Credit purchases | X |
| Purchases returns | X | | |
| Set-off/contra entries | X | | |
| Balance c/d | X | | |
| | X | | X |
| | | Balance b/d D | X |

The corresponding (opposite) entry of the set-off/contra is contained in the Sales ledger control account

## Purchases ledger control account entries and sources

| *Entry* | *Dr/Cr* | *Value is:* | *Source* |
|---|---|---|---|
| Balance b/d | Cr | Total amount owing to suppliers at the beginning of the period | Balance c/d from previous period |
| Credit purchases | Cr | Total amount (including VAT) invoiced by suppliers during the period | From 'total' column, Purchases day book |
| Payments to suppliers | Dr | Total value of money paid to suppliers during the period | From cash book - cash and bank columns |
| Settlement discount received | Dr | Total value of discount deducted when paying suppliers | From cash book |
| Purchases returns | Dr | Total value of credit notes (including VAT) received from suppliers during the period | From 'total' column, Purchases returns day book |
| Set-off/ contra entry | Dr | Where a supplier is also a customer and amounts owing are set against each other in the ledgers | Journal |

## reconciliation of purchases ledger control account and purchases ledger

If the double-entry has been completed correctly, the total of the subsidiary purchases ledger account balances should agree with the balance of the Purchases control account. These balances should be regularly **reconciled**. Possible reasons for discrepancies between the Purchases ledger control account balance and the total of purchases ledger balances could be caused by a number of errors:

**type of account entry**

credit purchases

purchases returns

payments to suppliers

settlement discount received

set-off

**possible cause of account error**

entry omitted

entry understated ('undercast')

entry made twice

entry too high ('overcast')

Note: not all errors come to light in a reconciliation: there could be double-entry errors that require correction – for example, a transaction entered in the wrong subsidiary purchases ledger account (error of commission) will not affect the balance reconciliation.

**EXAMPLE – purchases ledger reconciliation: dealing with errors**

The Purchases ledger control account balance is £37,082 but the total of the supplier account balances in the purchases ledger is £36,362. The net difference of £720 is the result of the following three errors in the control account:

| Errors in the Purchases ledger control account | Difference |
|---|---|
| 1. Set-off of £580 has not been posted to the control account | £580 |
| 2. Discount received of £320 credited to the control account | £640 |
| 3. The total column of the purchases day book is £16,772 but has been entered in the control account as £16,272 | £500 |

Amendments needed in the Purchases ledger control account are as follows:

| Purchases ledger control | | | |
|---|---|---|---|
| **1.** Set-off | 580 | Balance b/d | 37,082 |
| **2.** Discount received | 640 | **3.** Purchases day book | 500 |
| Balance c/d | 36,362 | | |
| | 37,582 | | 37,582 |
| | | Balance b/d | 36,362 |

**37,082 – 580 – 640 + 500 = 36,362**

Note: this example shows errors in the control account. Any errors in the purchases ledger accounts (eg payment posted to the wrong supplier account) must be corrected by entries within the ledger accounts and not in the control account.

## bank reconciliation

### reconciliation of the cash book (bank columns) to the bank statement

The bank account in the cash book **is not a control account**, but like control accounts it needs to be reconciled regularly – in this case to the business bank statement. Regular reconciliation will highlight any errors or discrepancies and explain any differences.

Possible reasons for discrepancies between the cash book bank balance and the bank statement balance include:

| *Timing differences:* | *Description* | *Action required* |
|---|---|---|
| Unpresented cheques | Cheques issued and entered in the cash book but not yet appearing on the bank statements | Enter in reconciliation statement |
| Outstanding lodgements | Receipts entered into the cash book but not yet appearing on the bank statement | Enter in reconciliation statement |
| *Other reasons:* | | |
| Items on the bank statements but not yet entered in the cash book | ▪ Receipts from customers<br>▪ Direct debit or standing order payments<br>▪ Returned customer cheques<br>▪ Bank charges and interest | Update the cash book with the new entries |
| Double-entry errors | Error in bookkeeping entries | Journal entry |

**EXAMPLE – reconcilation of cash book to bank statement**

The bank balance in the cash book is £11,482 debit (money in the bank).

The closing balance on the bank statement is a credit of £8,662 (a debit in the cash book).

The following errors or differences have been identified:

1. There is an outstanding lodgement of £2,540
2. A direct debit of £550 has not been entered in the cash book
3. A BACS receipt of £1,410 from a customer has been entered in the cash book as £1,140.

The amendments needed in the cash book are as follows:

| Bank | | | |
|---|---|---|---|
| Balance b/d | 11,482 | **2.** Direct debit | 550 |
| **3.** Customer receipt | 270 | Balance c/d | 11,202 |
| | 11,752 | | 11,752 |
| Balance b/d | 11,202 | | |

The corrected bank balance in the cash book is now £11,202 but this is still not the same as the balance on the bank statement of £8,662. The lodgement of £2,540 (difference 1) has not yet reached the bank so must be deducted from the cash book balance to reconcile the figures as follows: Bank statement balance £8,662 + outstanding lodgement £2,540 = Cash book balance £11,202

# 12 Errors

## *HOW TO DEAL WITH BOOKKEEPING ERRORS*

*Errors happen. You will need to know about how they affect the accounts, how to deal with them and correct them. As they are non-regular transactions they are corrected by journal entry. They may also affect the stated profit in the statements.*

*Some errors are not revealed by the trial balance and some are.*

**errors not revealed by the trial balance**

**these errors are:**

- error of principle
- error of commission
- error of original entry
- error of omission
- reversal of entries
- compensating error

**errors revealed by the trial balance:**

A trial balance will not balance if any of these bookkeeping errors are made:

- only one entry made
- both entries on same side
- for different (unequal) amounts
- error in transfer of balance to trial balance
- balance omitted from trial balance

## errors that are NOT revealed by the trial balance

| error | description | treatment in journal |
|---|---|---|
| **error of principle** | transaction is entered in the wrong class of account | transfer the value from one account to the other |
| **error of commission** | transaction is entered in the wrong account, typically in the subsidiary sales or purchase ledgers | transfer the value within the subsidiary ledger, but debit and credit the control accounts in the journal |
| **error of original entry** | wrong value is entered in the accounts (but correct double entry) | remove the error and make the correct entry |
| **error of omission** | transaction is omitted completely from the accounts | enter the transaction in full |
| **reversal of entries** | debit and credit entries are reversed | remove the error and make the correct entry |
| **compensating error** | two errors are made that balance each other out | remove the errors and make the correct entries |

## suspense account

If a trial balance fails to balance, the difference between the two columns (Dr and Cr) is posted to a Suspense account until the reason for the imbalance (difference in value) is discovered and a correction (or corrections) made.

**EXAMPLE – using the suspense account to correct errors**

The debit column of a trial balance totals £200,000 and the credit column totals £198,000. There is an imbalance (difference in value) of £2,000 (ie £200,000 – £198,000) resulting in a shortage on the credit side.

This is put right by posting the £2,000 to the credit side of the Suspense account, resulting in the trial balance now balancing with totals of £200,000. See below.

| Trial Balance | | |
|---|---|---|
| | *total debit balances (£)* 200,000 | *total credit balances (£)* 198,000 |
| Suspense account | | 2,000 |
| New totals | 200,000 | 200,000 |

| Suspense Account | |
|---|---|
| *Dr (£)* | *Cr (£)* |
| | 2,000 |

## errors that ARE revealed by the trial balance

| error | description | treatment in journal |
|---|---|---|
| **one-sided principle** | only one side (debit or credit) of the transaction entered | enter the missing entry and post the other side to Suspense |
| **both entries on the same side** | instead of a debit and a credit, two debits or two credits have been entered | remove one of the duplicated entries and post the other side to Suspense |
| **entries of different amounts** | the debit and credit entries do not balance | remove the incorrect entry, post the other side to Suspense then make the correct entry and post the other side to Suspense |
| **error in balance transfer to trial balance** | an incorrect balance figure is transferred to the trial balance | |
| **balance omitted from trial balance** | an account balance is not transferred to the trial balance | enter the missing balance and post the other side to Suspense |

## the need to correct errors

One important requirement of accounting is that financial statements should be 'free from error'. This is part of the concept of 'faithful representation' which states that accounting information should be reliable, truthful and unbiased.

This means that any errors discovered **at any time** in the accounting process must be corrected. This is particularly important when it comes to **profit**.

Any **errors found after profit has already been calculated** must be corrected.

## the effect of different types of error on profit calculations

| **error corrections which increase profit** | **error corrections which reduce profit** |
|---|---|
| income under-stated | income over-stated |
| purchases over-stated | purchases under-stated |
| opening inventory overvalued | opening inventory undervalued |
| closing inventory undervalued | closing inventory overvalued |
| expense over-stated | expense under-stated |

## the journal – a summary and a reminder

The journal is a book of prime entry. It is used to record transactions that do not belong in any other book of prime entry. It is written evidence of the sequence of transactions (the 'audit trail') from source document to financial statements. It is used to record 'non-regular transactions' which include:

- period-end or year-end adjustments:
  - accruals and prepayments
  - depreciation
  - allowance for doubtful debts
  - closing inventory
- period-end or year-end transfers
- purchase and sale of non-current assets
- write-off of irrecoverable debts
- correction of errors

## correction of errors in the journal – 4 line or 2 line entries?

The 4 line journal uses the **error amount** to remove an incorrect entry and then enter a correct entry (ie 2 debits and 2 credits). An alternative is to post to the journal for the **difference**, resulting in a 2 line journal with one debit and one credit.

# 13 Year-end transfer journals

## *DEALING WITH THE ADJUSTMENTS*

*The extended trial balance is used to move account balances from the initial trial balance to the financial statements, and to enter any period-end adjustments. Any adjustments and transfers must also be entered in the book of prime entry for non-regular transactions: the journal.*

### year-end adjustments

The period-end adjustments listed below are entered as journals in the relevant accounts. The revised account balances are then transferred by journal to the statement of profit or loss and to the relevant accounts in the statement of financial position.

- accruals of income and expenses
- prepayments of income and expenses
- depreciation of non-current assets
- irrecoverable debts
- allowance for doubtful debts
- closing inventory

## reminder notes on the statement of profit or loss

The statement of profit or loss is a double-entry 'T' account in its own right.

Expenses are debited and income credited to arrive at a balance which represents the profit or loss for the period:

- a credit balance brought down = profit
- a debit balance brought down = loss

The statement of profit or loss account balance appears in the statement of financial position as profit (or loss) for the period.

## year-end transfers to the statement of profit or loss

All income and expense account balances at the end of the period are closed off and transferred to the statement of profit or loss.

**EXAMPLE**

To transfer Sales account balance:

| | |
|---|---|
| Debit | Sales account |
| Credit | statement of profit or loss |

**EXAMPLE**

To transfer Wages account balance:

| | |
|---|---|
| Debit | statement of profit or loss |
| Credit | Wages account |

# 14 Memory aids

## KEEPING YOUR MEMORY FIT

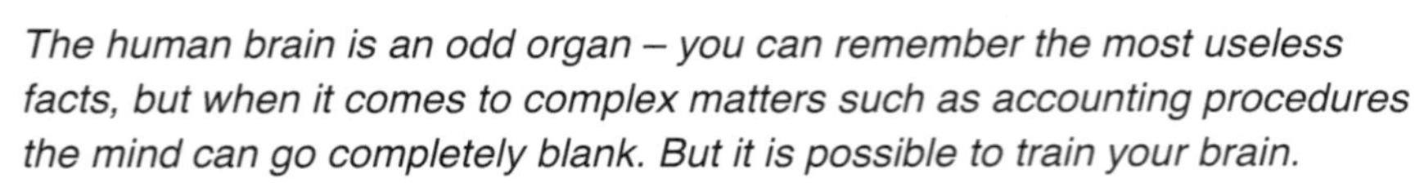

*The human brain is an odd organ – you can remember the most useless facts, but when it comes to complex matters such as accounting procedures the mind can go completely blank. But it is possible to train your brain.*

*At the beginning of this Guide there are some revision tips which suggest that you can study effectively and recall information by . . .*

- ***Observing**, ie remembering what information looks like on the page, using diagrams, lists, mind-maps and colour coding. Memory is very visual.*
- ***Writing** information down, using flash cards, post-it notes, notes on a phone. It is the actual process of writing which helps to fix the information in the brain.*
- ***Learning** by regularly going through your course notes and text books. Find a 'study buddy' in your class (or online) to teach and test each other as the course progresses.*

- ***Chill out*** *when you get tired. Give your brain a chance to recover. Get some exercise and fresh air, work out. In the ancient world there was the saying that a fit body was usually home to a fit mind.*
- ***Treats*** *– promise yourself rewards when you have finished studying – meet friends, eat chocolate, have a drink, listen to music.*

## *exam preparation*

- ***Practice, practice, practice*** *when preparing for your assessment.*

  *Practice the questions and assessments in the Osborne Books workbooks.*

  *Practice the free online assessments on the Osborne Books website:*

  *Go to* www.osbornebooks.co.uk/aat_accounting_qcf *or scan this code . . . .*

## *using the memory aids*

*On the next few pages are blank spaces for you to set out ways of remembering many of the definitions and formulas needed for your AAT assessment.*

# some aids to memory

On the next few pages are blank spaces for you to set out some of the important accounting entries and definitions you will need to memorise for your assessment.

## ACCRUALS AND PREPAYMENTS

Enter the accounting entries you will need for the following:

| **Accrued expense** | **Accrued income** |
| --- | --- |
| **Prepaid expense** | **Prepaid income** |

## DEALING WITH ALLOWANCES FOR DOUBTFUL DEBTS

Write in the blank boxes in the table below for each of the transactions listed on the left:

- the name of the account debited (first blank column) and credited (second blank column)
- the name of the financial statement in which the each entry appears (ie SPL or SFP)

| | debit/financial statement | credit/financial statement |
|---|---|---|
| **creating an allowance for doubtful debts for the first time** | | |
| **increasing the allowance for doubtful debts in a subsequent period** | | |
| **decreasing the allowance for doubtful debts in a subsequent period** | | |

## DEALING WITH INVENTORY

Write down the accounting entries for opening inventory and closing inventory.

| Opening inventory | Closing inventory |
|---|---|
| | |

Write down a definition of each of these three different methods of inventory valuation.

| FIFO | AVCO | LIFO |
|---|---|---|
| | | |

Write in the correct column below the errors that **are** revealed and those that are **not** revealed by a trial balance.

| Errors revealed by a trial balance | Errors not revealed by a trial balance |
| --- | --- |
| | |

# index